I0791435
THE SWAN
HAS ABOUT
25,000 FEATHERS
IN ITS BODY.

SWAN EGGS
TAKE BETWEEN
35 AND 42 DAYS
TO HATCH.

THE SWAN HAS LONG
REPRESENTED
ELEGANCE AND REFINEMENT.

TRUMPETER
SWAN
TRUMPETER SWANS ARE THE LARGEST
NATIVE WATERFOWL AND THE HEAVIEST
FLYING BIRDS IN NORTH AMERICA.

NOTED FOR THEIR
GRACEFULNESS
IN THE WATER,
SWANS HAVE BEEN
THE SUBJECT OF MANY
POEMS, FAIRY TALES,
LEGENDS, AND
MUSICAL WORKS.

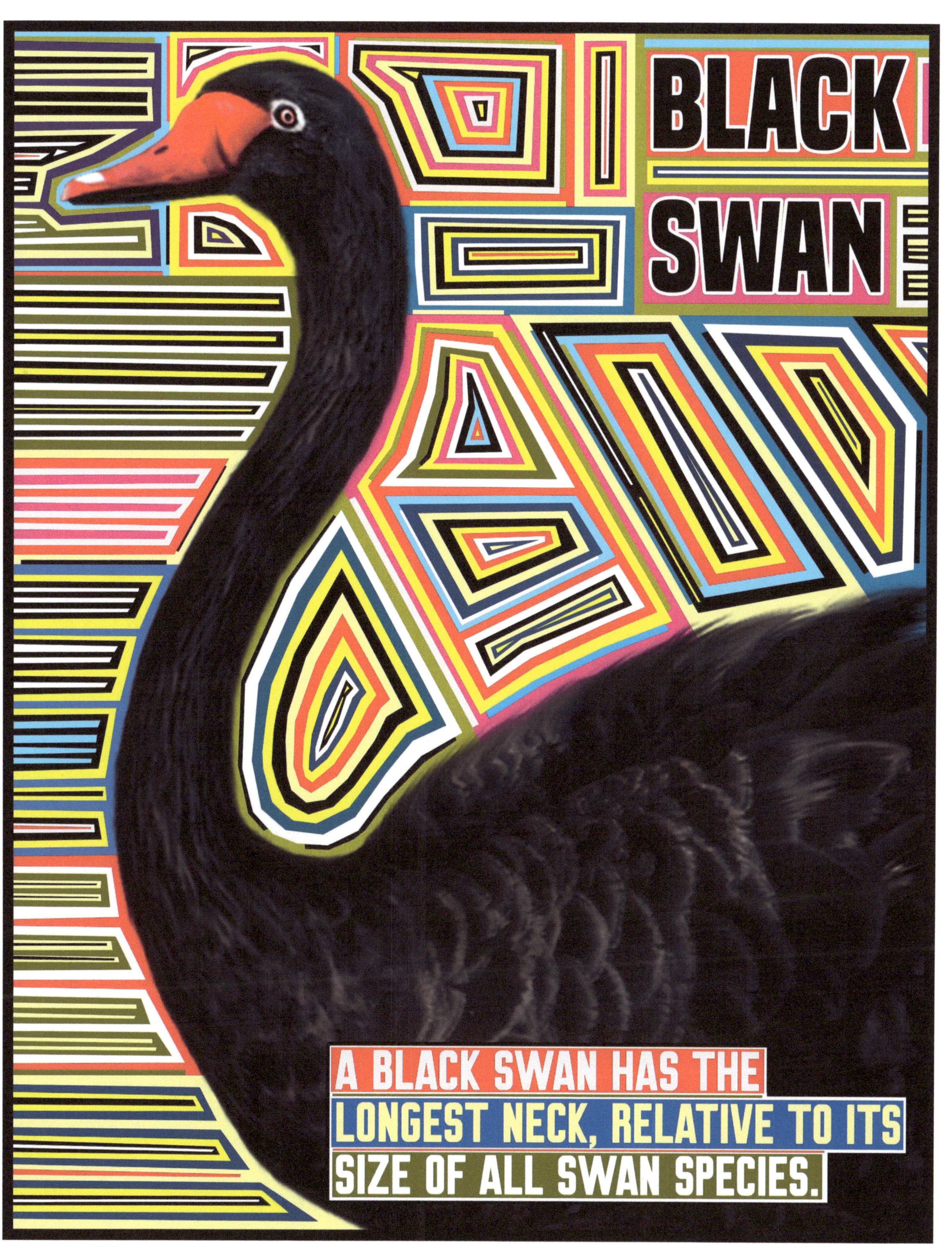
BLACK
SWAN
A BLACK SWAN HAS THE
LONGEST NECK, RELATIVE TO ITS
SIZE OF ALL SWAN SPECIES.

SWANS ARE CLOSE
RELATIVES WITH
GEESE AND DUCKS.

THERE ARE SIX DIFFERENT SPECIES OF SWANS.

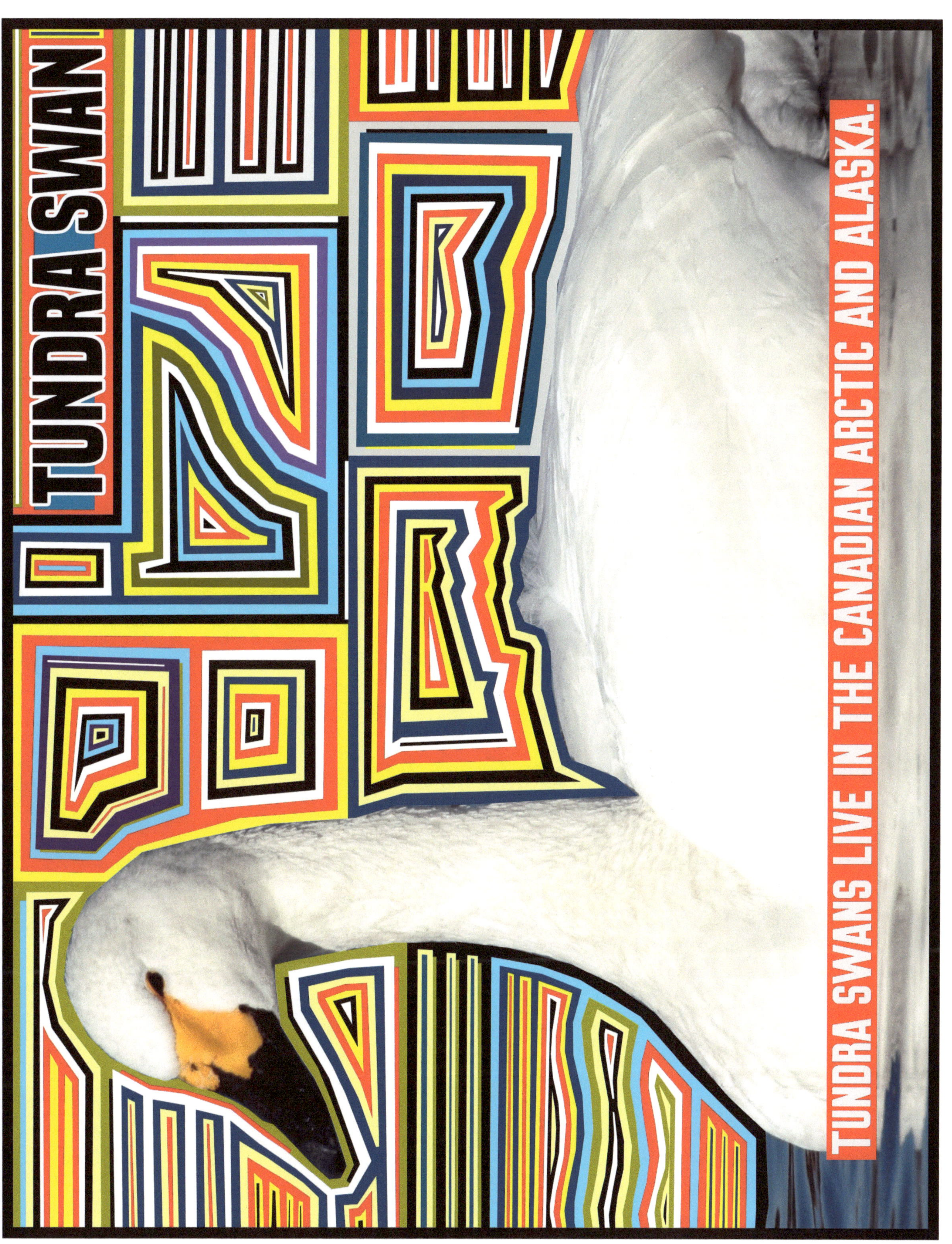

TUNDRA SWAN
TUNDRA SWANS LIVE IN THE CANADIAN ARCTIC AND ALASKA.

SWANS ARE VERY INTELLIGENT AND REMEMBER WHO HAS BEEN NICE TO THEM, OR NOT.

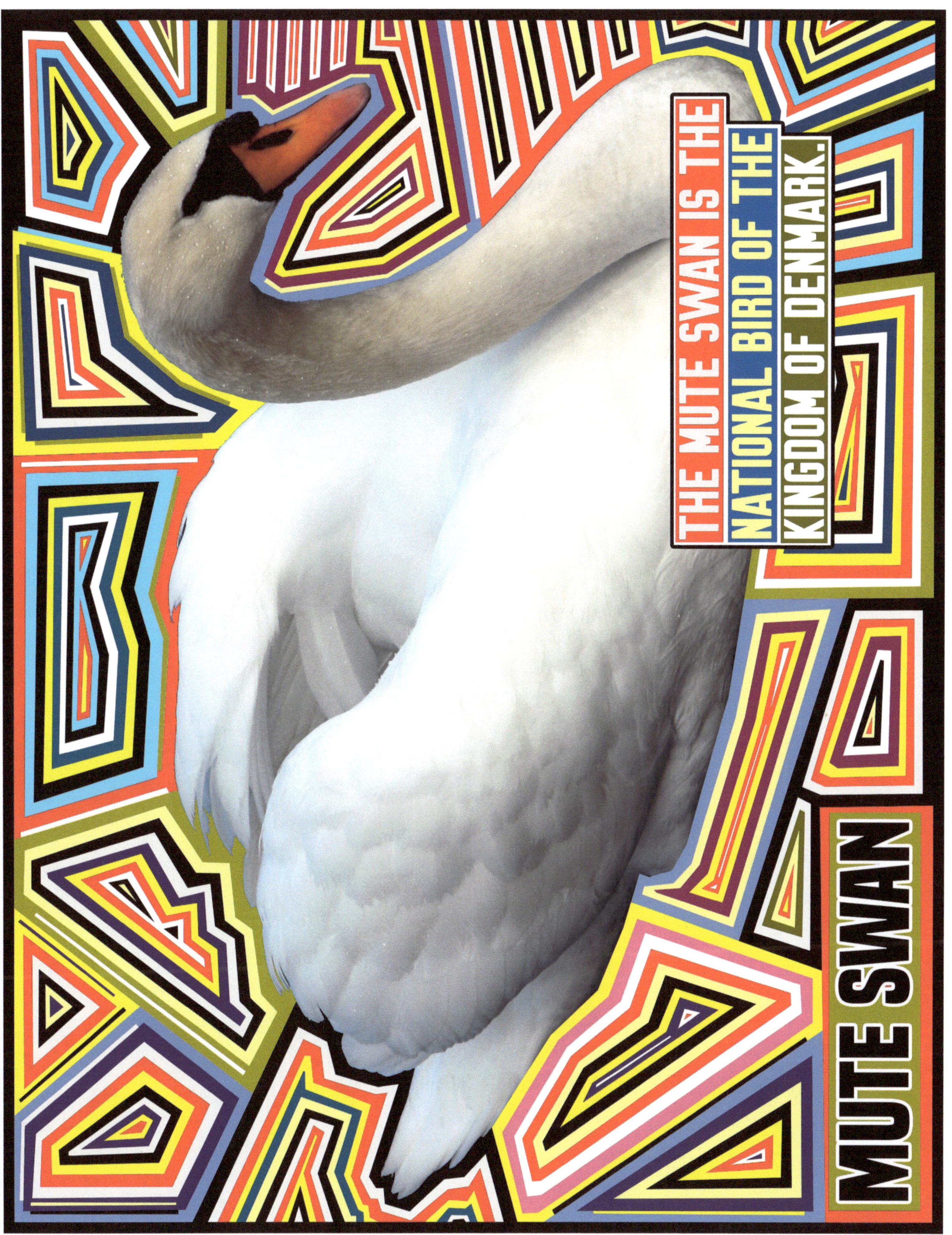

THE MUTE SWAN IS THE NATIONAL BIRD OF THE KINGDOM OF DENMARK.
MUTE SWAN

CYGNOPHOBIA OR KIKNOPHOBIA IS THE FEAR OF SWANS.

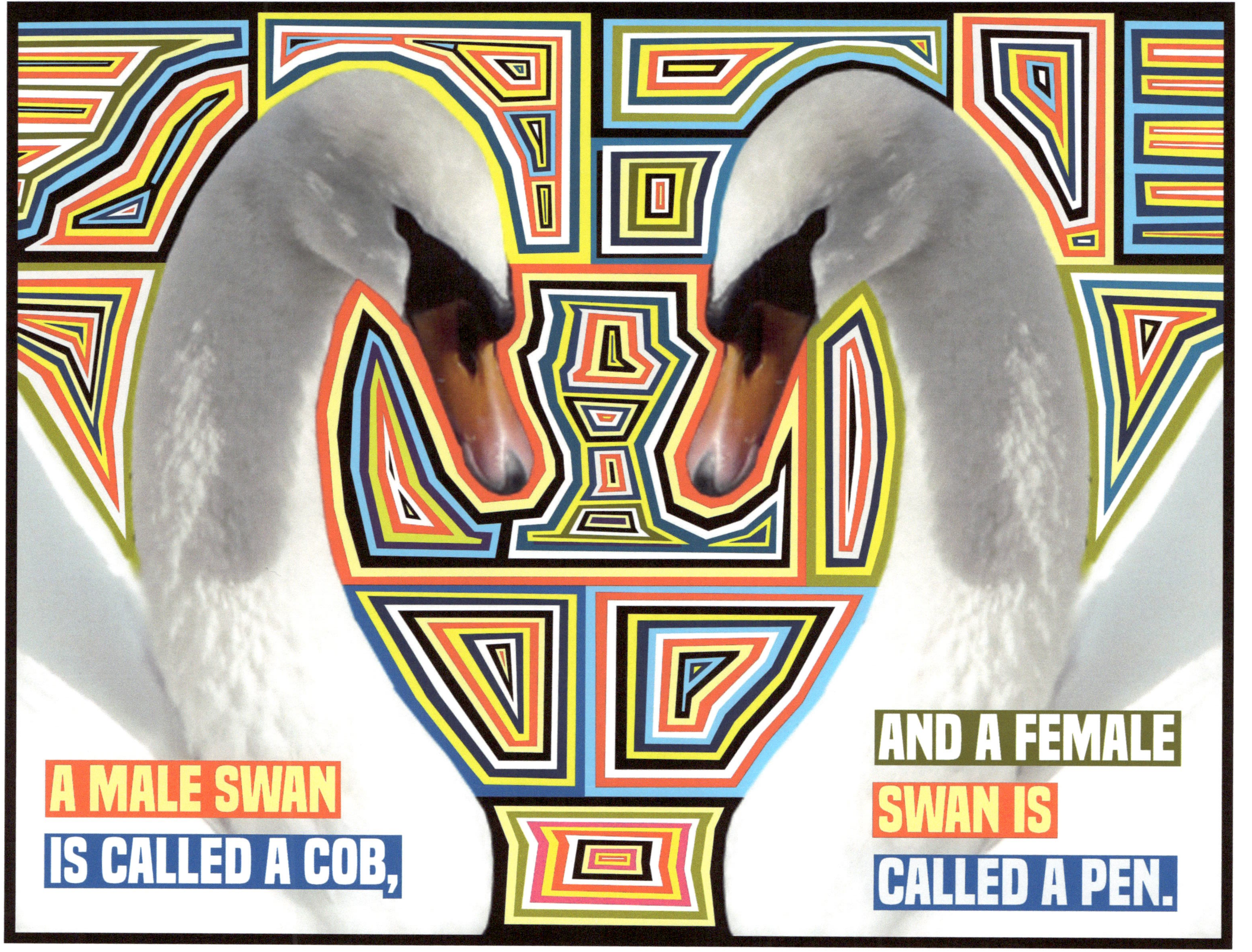
A MALE SWAN
IS CALLED A COB,
AND A FEMALE
SWAN IS
CALLED A PEN.

BLACK SWANS
ARE NATIVE
TO AUSTRALIA.

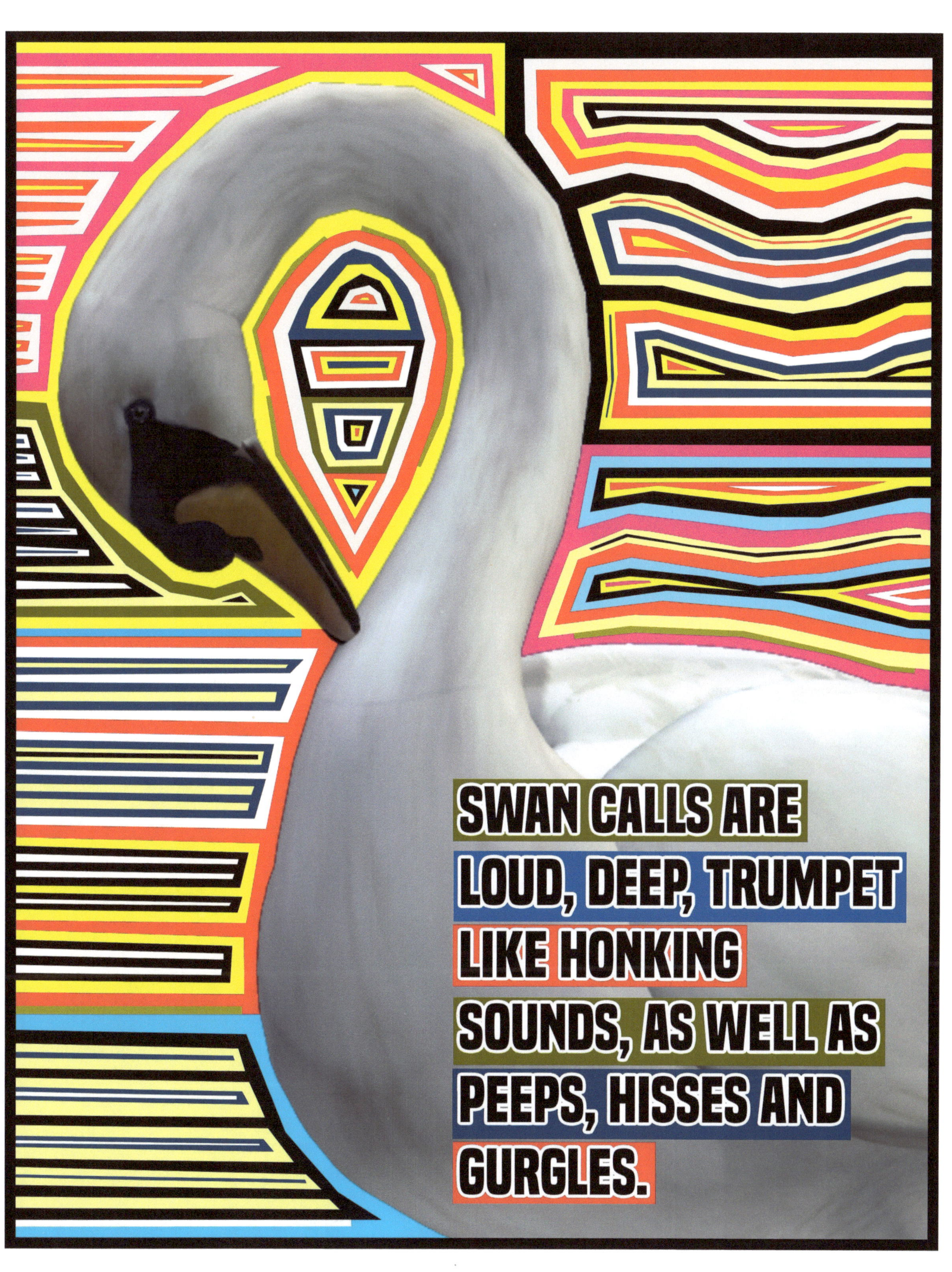

SWAN CALLS ARE LOUD, DEEP, TRUMPET LIKE HONKING SOUNDS, AS WELL AS PEEPS, HISSES AND GURGLES.

SWANS CAN FLY AS FAST
AS 60 MILES PER HOUR!

WHOOPER SWAN
THE WHOOPER SWAN'S NAME IS A REFERENCE TO ITS LOUD "WHOOPING" CALL. IT IS FINLAND'S NATIONAL BIRD.

A GROUP OF WILD SWANS IS KNOWN AS A HERD, A GROUP IN CAPTIVITY IS CALLED A FLEET.

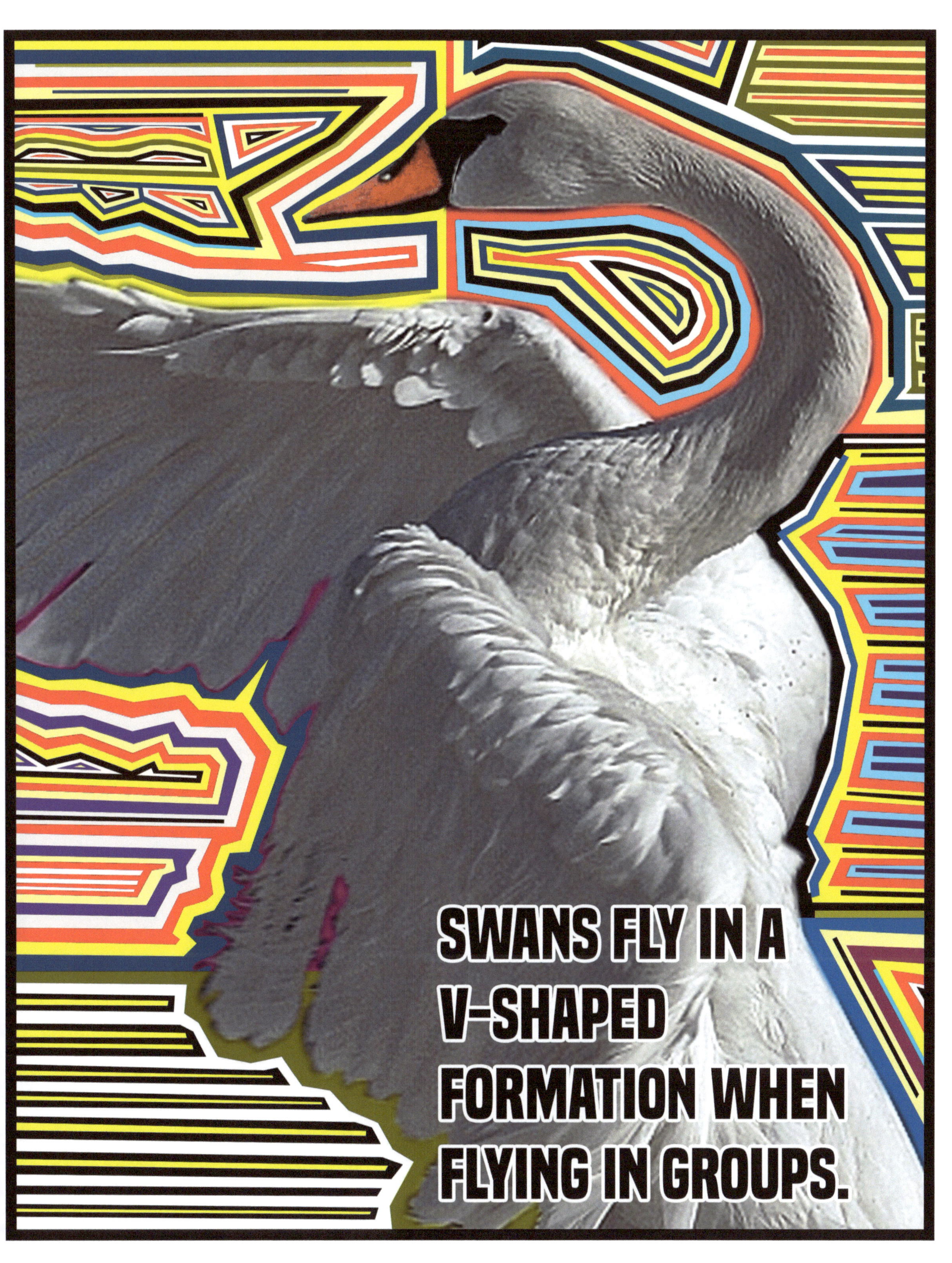
SWANS FLY IN A V-SHAPED FORMATION WHEN FLYING IN GROUPS.

DUE TO THEIR LARGE
SIZE, SWANS HAVE
FEW NATURAL
PREDATORS IN THE WILD.

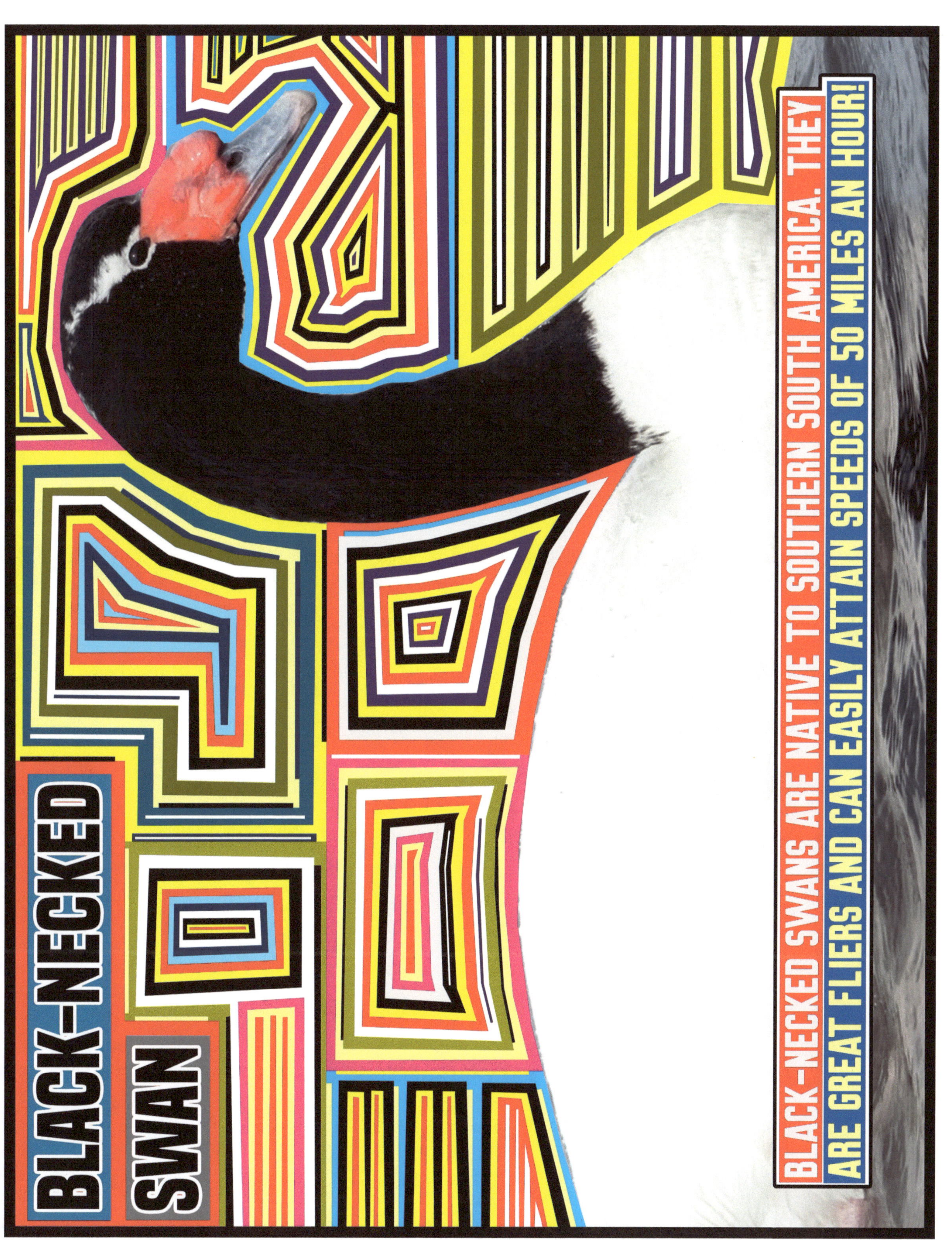

BLACK-NECKED
SWAN
BLACK-NECKED SWANS ARE NATIVE TO SOUTHERN SOUTH AMERICA. THEY ARE GREAT FLIERS AND CAN EASILY ATTAIN SPEEDS OF 50 MILES AN HOUR!

SWANS ARE AMONG
THE LARGEST FLYING BIRDS.

SWANS WILL MATE FOR LIFE.

THE END.
THANK YOU.

COPYRIGHT 2020
BY EDDIE ALFARO
ALL RIGHTS RESERVED.

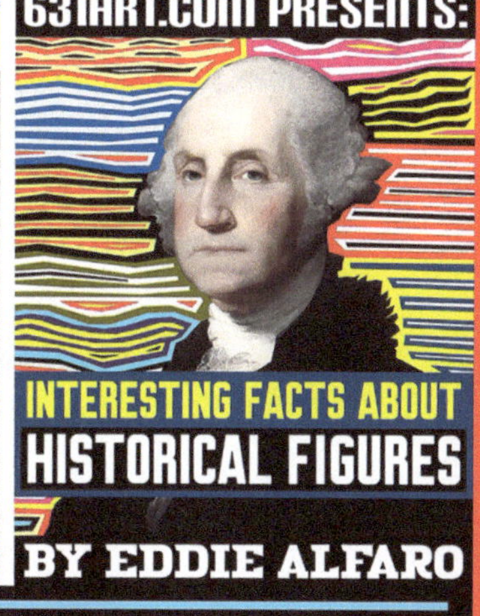

MORE BOOKS AT:

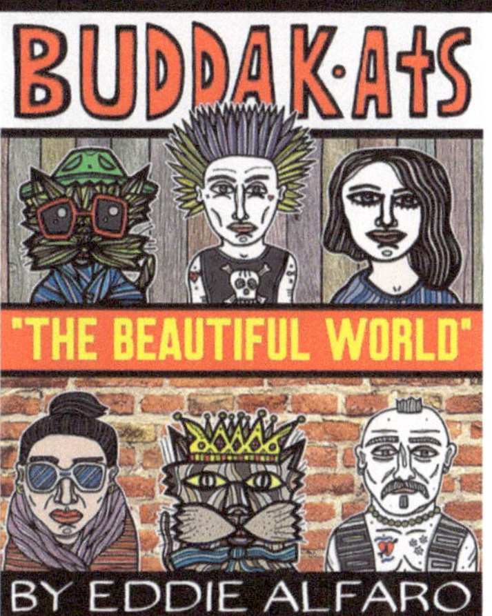

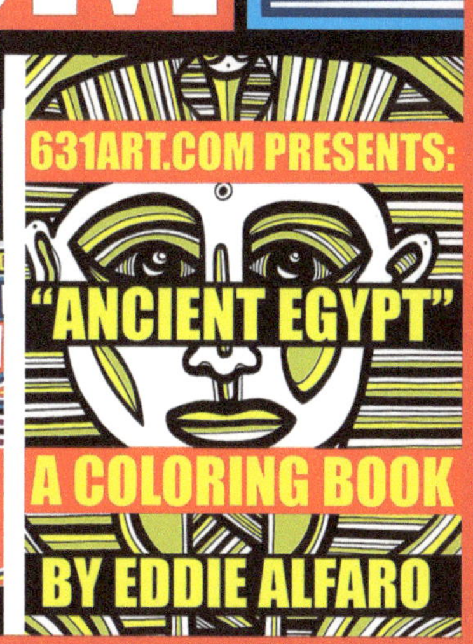